The Primary Source Library of Famous Explorers™

Francisco Pizarro

A Primary Source Biography

Lynn Hoogenboom

The Rosen Publishing Group's

PowerKids Press™

PRIMARY SOURCE

New York

For Jan

Published in 2006 by The Rosen Publishing Group, Inc.
29 East 21st Street, New York, NY 10010

First Edition

Editor: Daryl Heller
Book Design: Albert B. Hanner
Layout Design: Greg Tucker
Photo Researcher: Amy Feinberg

Special thanks to Mr. John Buellens for the translation on page 21.

Photo Credits: Cover Réunion des Musées Nationaux/Art Resource, NY; p. 5 (top) © Topham/The Image Works, (bottom) map by Greg Tucker; p. 6 (top) Library of Congress Geography and Map Division, (bottom), p. 19 (top) The Art Archive/Biblioteca Nazionale Marciana Venice/Dagli Orti; p. 9 (top) © Hulton Archive/Getty Images, (bottom) © ANA/The Image Works; p. 10 (top) British Library, London, UK/Bridgeman Art Library, (bottom), p. 12 (bottom), p. 15 (bottom), p. 16 (bottom) Bildarchiv Preussischer Kulturbesitz/Art Resource, NY; p. 12 (top), p. 16 (top) The Art Archive/Archaeological Museum Lima/Dagli Orti; p. 15 (top) © Jim Erickson/Corbis; p. 19 (bottom) Werner Forman/Art Resource, NY; p. 21 Rare Books Division, The New York Public Library, Astor, Lenox and Tilden Foundations.

Library of Congress Cataloging-in-Publication Data

Hoogenboom, Lynn.
  Francisco Pizarro : a primary source biography / Lynn Hoogenboom.
    p. cm. — (The primary source library of famous explorers)
  Includes index.
  ISBN 1-4042-3038-6 (library binding)
  1. Pizarro, Francisco, ca. 1475–1541—Juvenile literature. 2. Peru—History—Conquest, 1522–1548—Juvenile literature. 3. Incas—Juvenile literature. 4. South America—Discovery and exploration—Spanish—Juvenile literature. 5. Explorers—South America—Biography—Juvenile literature. 6. Explorers—Spain—Biography—Juvenile literature. I. Title.

  F3442.P776H66 2006
  985'.02'092—dc22

                        2005001479

Manufactured in the United States of America

Contents

The Early Years

Francisco Pizarro lived during a time of great change. In 1492, when Pizarro was about 18 years old, Christopher Columbus became the first European to discover the Americas, which Europeans called the New World. After that other lands were discovered nearly every year.

Little is known about Pizarro's early life. He was born in Trujillo, Spain, around 1475. His father was Gonzalo Pizarro, who was a military officer. His mother was Francisca Gonzales, who came from a poor family. Pizarro's parents never married.

Like most poor children at that time, Pizarro did not go to school. He never learned to read or write. At some point Pizarro left Spain and moved to Hispaniola, the Caribbean island where Columbus started the first Spanish **colony** in the New World. The first record of Pizarro is in 1510, when he was one of the 300 **settlers** who traveled with the **explorer** Alonso de Ojeda from Hispaniola to start a colony on the coast of South America.

Pizarro did not have a happy childhood. Instead of attending school, he worked as a swineherd. A swineherd was a person who took care of boars that were kept as livestock. A boar is a type of wild pig.

The small map below shows the path Francisco Pizarro and other Spanish settlers took when they sailed from Spain to Hispaniola in the early 1500s. The large map shows the areas of Central America and South America that Pizarro explored in the 1520s and the 1530s.

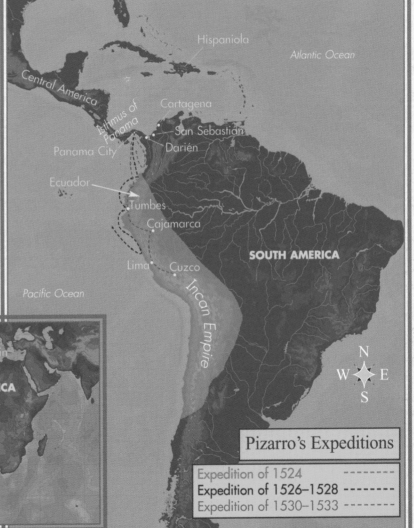

Central America

Hispaniola

Atlantic Ocean

Cartagena

Isthmus of Panama

San Sebastian

Panama City

Darién

Ecuador

Tumbes

Cajamarca

SOUTH AMERICA

Lima

Cuzco

Incan Empire

Pacific Ocean

N
W   E
S

Pizarro's Expeditions

Expedition of 1524 — — — — —
Expedition of 1526–1528 — — — —
Expedition of 1530–1533 — — — —

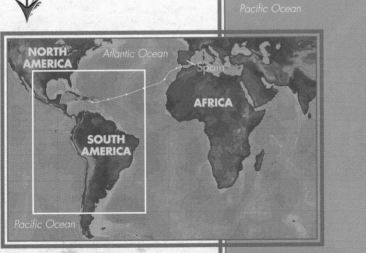

NORTH AMERICA

Atlantic Ocean

Spain

AFRICA

SOUTH AMERICA

Pacific Ocean

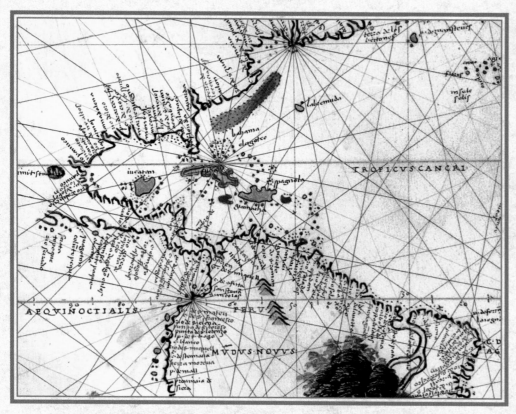

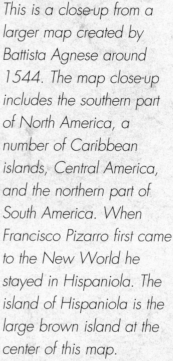

This is a close-up from a larger map created by Battista Agnese around 1544. The map close-up includes the southern part of North America, a number of Caribbean islands, Central America, and the northern part of South America. When Francisco Pizarro first came to the New World he stayed in Hispaniola. The island of Hispaniola is the large brown island at the center of this map.

This picture from the 1500s shows Spanish soldiers fighting Indians on the coast of America. The Spanish often attacked the Indians. They tried to steal the Indians' food and to capture men and women. These captives would be used as slaves.

Ojeda's Settlement

Ojeda and his settlers landed on the South American coast near modern-day Cartagena, Colombia. They soon attacked an Indian village. The Indians killed 69 settlers with poisoned arrows and drove the Spanish away.

Ojeda and his men moved west to the shore of the Gulf of Uraba in modern-day Colombia. Ojeda called this spot San Sebastián. After some trouble with the Indians, Ojeda left Pizarro in charge and sailed for help. Ojeda was **shipwrecked**, however, and could not return. After several months Pizarro and his men tried to sail for Hispaniola. They had to land near Cartagena when one of their boats sank. Martín Fernández de Enciso, a **partner** of Ojeda's, saved the group. Enciso ordered the settlers to return with him to San Sebastián. However, the Indians had burned the Spaniards' **fort**. Vasco Núñez de Balboa, who had come on Enciso's ship, heard that the Indians on the other side of the gulf were friendlier. There the settlers started the town of Darién, on Colombia's coast, near modern-day Panama.

The Discovery of the Pacific Ocean

Balboa, who became Darién's governor, heard from the Indians that over the mountains there was another sea and a gold-filled land. He planned an **expedition**. Pizarro was one of his captains. On September 1, 1513, about 190 Spaniards and their Indian guides crossed the **Isthmus** of Panama, which connects North America and South America. On September 25, they climbed a mountain. Near the top Balboa told his men to stay back, so he could be the first European to view this new sea. This sea is now known as the Pacific Ocean. The group returned to Darién.

Meanwhile, Charles V, king of Spain, had sent a new governor to Darién. Pedro Arias Dávila, called Pedrarias, arrived on June 29, 1514. Pedrarias thought Balboa was planning a **rebellion** and ordered Pizarro to arrest Balboa. In a **trial** Balboa was found **guilty** of **treason** and was killed. In 1519, Pedrarias built a city on the west coast of modern-day Panama that was called Panama City. This became the new capital.

Antonio de Herrera was a Spanish historian. He wrote about Balboa's 1513 discovery of the Pacific Ocean around 1600. In his book Herrera wrote that when Balboa first looked down on the Pacific, he raised his arms and thanked God for his discovery. The Spaniards who traveled with him soon did the same. Their Native American guides were curious as to why the sight of the ocean should cause the Spanish such joy.

The Isthmus of Panama is in Central America. Because there is so much heat and heavy rain in the area, there is a rain forest. Balboa and his men are shown climbing the hills of the rain forest around 1513.

Panama is only 45 miles (72 km) wide where Balboa crossed it. The crossing was still hard. The jungle, or rain forest, was so thick that Balboa and his men could not see the sky. To get through the lakes and swamps, or wetlands, they had to take all their clothes off and carry them on their heads. Bugs bit them all the time.

9

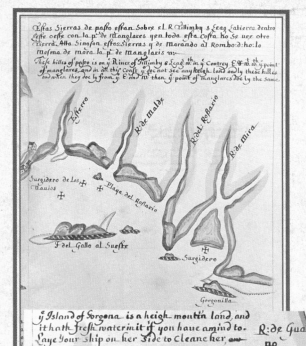

Estas Sierras de passo estan sobre el R. Tillimby s Eras Latierra dentro Leste oeste con la p. de Manglares yen toda esta Costa ho Se uez otro Tierra Alta Sinoson estros Sierras y de Morando al Rombo:d:ho:lo mesma de mora la p. de manglaris un...

These hilles of passo is on y River of Tillimby s Lias m. in y Contrey E F m. w y point of manglares and in all this Coast y do not see any heigh land only these hilles and when they doe ly from y E and W then y point of manglares doe ly the same.

Pizarro · R. de Maldo · Rdel. Rosario · R. de Mira

Surgidero de los Clauios · Playa del Rosario

F. del Gallo al Suestr · Surgidero

Gorgonilla

y Island of Gorgona is a heigh moutin land, and it hath fresh water in it if you haue a mind to Laye Your ship on her side to Cleane her, ... · R: de Gua po

Sierra de Largo...
The Island...

An Englishman made this map around 1685. He copied his map from a 1669 Spanish map. The Spanish map was based on notes taken by a Spanish explorer. Gallo Island, at center left, is where Pizarro stayed in 1527. Other islands, such as the Island of Gorgona at center right, were included on this map.

From a 1685 Explorer's Map

"Island of Gorgona is a heigh moutin land, and it hath fresh water in it if you have a mind to Laye your ship on her side to Cleane her . . ."

This means that Gorgona had mountains and drinking water. Ships could stop there to be cleaned or repaired.

When Governor Pedro de los Rios sent a ship to Gallo Island to take Pizarro and his men back to Panama City, Pizarro drew a line in the sand with his sword. He pointed south and said, "This is the way to Peru, the way to glory and riches." Then he pointed north and said, "There lies Panama, desertion, and poverty. Choose. . . ." Pizarro told his men that those who remained would be rich. Those who returned to Panama would stay poor.

In this 1500s painting, Francisco Pizarro, Diego de Almagro, and Father Hernando de Luque are shown planning their exploration of Peru, where they hoped to find gold.

The Search for Peru

In 1522, Pizarro and two partners decided to find the gold-filled land that Balboa had heard about. Pizarro would lead the expedition, Father Hernando de Luque would raise money, and Diego de Almagro would find supplies. Three times between 1524 and 1527, they tried to find the land that people in Panama had started to call Peru.

During the second trip, the crew of one of Pizarro's ships saw an Indian raft filled with beautiful things near modern-day Ecuador. Pizarro needed more supplies before he could take his men there. They waited on an island near Ecuador. Almagro tried to get more men and supplies. The new governor of Panama, Pedro de los Rios, thought too many men had been killed trying to find Peru. He tried to bring Pizarro and his men back, but Pizarro refused. Seven months later the governor let Almagro send a supply boat. Pizarro sailed south to Tumbes **Harbor**, which was part of Peru. Pizarro did not have enough men to attack, so he gave the Indians presents and pretended to be friendly.

This picture from around 1587 shows Francisco Pizarro gathering soldiers in Spain for his conquest of Peru. Almagro did not go to Spain with Pizarro in 1528. However, the Peruvian artist Poma de Ayala drew Almagro on the left. Pizarro is on the right.

This 1596 picture shows Francisco Pizarro in the Spanish court of King Charles V in 1528. The explorer Hernán Cortés returned to Spain in 1528 with riches he had taken from Mexico. Charles V allowed Pizarro to attack Peru because he hoped Pizarro would find riches there as well.

A Trip to Spain

When Pizarro returned to Panama, everyone was **excited** to hear about Tumbes, a rich city Pizarro had found on the edge of Peru. Governor Rios, however, refused to let Pizarro make another **voyage**. Pizarro and his partners, Father Luque and Diego de Almagro, decided that one of them should go to Spain and get permission from the king. Pizarro looked and spoke well, so he was chosen.

Francisco Pizarro sailed for Spain in 1528. After he arrived he met with King Charles V. On July 16, 1529, the king gave Pizarro a royal **license** to **conquer** Peru. Pizarro found about 100 men in Spain to help with the conquest. Four of them were his half brothers. When Pizarro and his brothers arrived in America, his partners were angry. The king's license had made Pizarro governor of Peru and commander of its armed forces. After a long talk, Pizarro promised to share the gold equally with his partners. He also promised to ask the king to give Almagro a separate territory to rule after Peru was conquered.

The Inca

While Francisco Pizarro was preparing to attack Peru in 1530, things were going on inside the Incan **Empire** that would make the conquest easier. The Incan Empire reached from what is today southern Colombia through Ecuador, Peru, Bolivia, northern Chile, and northern Argentina. After Pizarro had left Peru in 1527, a deadly **disease** had spread through the empire. It was probably a European disease that some of the Inca caught from Pizarro's men when they visited Tumbes. More than 100,000 people died, including Huayna Capac, the **supreme** Inca.

Before he died Huayna Capac divided, or split, his kingdom, rather than leaving it to one son. The largest part went to Huascar, a son by his queen. He gave a smaller part to Atahuallpa, his favorite son, whose mother was one of Huayna Capac's other wives. Huascar was angry and went to war with Atahuallpa. Atahuallpa won the War of Two Brothers. He took over the part of the Incan Empire that Huascar had controlled.

 Machu Picchu is an ancient Incan city in the Andes mountains of Peru. Archaeologists, or people who study ruins to learn how earlier peoples lived, uncovered Machu Picchu in the early 1900s. Ruins are what is left of buildings after much time has passed.

 Atahuallpa was the thirteenth and final supreme Inca, or the last Incan king. This painting of him was done in the 1500s. The Inca believed their ruler was blessed because he was the favorite child of the Sun. All Inca prayed to the Sun.

There was no money in the Incan Empire because the government made sure everyone had what they needed. The government also gave everyone a job. Many people worked as farmers. Crops were often grown on terraces, or flat areas that were like extra large steps cut into the mountain. The Inca did not read or write. They kept records with a quipu, a long rope with different colored strings. Knots, or ties, on a string might tell how many people lived in a village or how much food it produced.

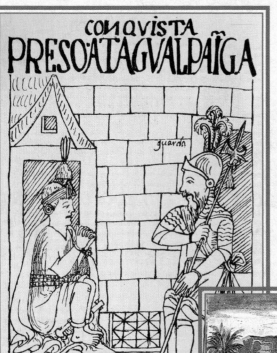

CONQVISTA
PRESO·ATAGVALPAINGA

guarda

preso ataqualpa en la cindad de caxam...
atnqualpa yriga dixo adon fran pizarro q les...
dixo q no sauia y dixo q les ycun sol dado yles ó...

In this picture from around 1587, Atahuallpa is held captive by the Spanish. Pizarro kept Atahuallpa alive because he wanted the supreme Inca to continue giving orders to his people. However, the person who would really be coming up with these orders was Francisco Pizarro.

Atahuallpa brought along thousands of soldiers for his meeting with Pizarro. Theodore de Bry's 1596 painting shows the supreme Inca being carried by his men. Historians say that Atahuallpa came to the meeting atop a golden throne. He wore a necklace made of emeralds, a type of prized green stone.

Conquest

On December 27, 1530, Francisco Pizarro sailed from Panama City to Peru to conquer it. When he reached Tumbes, however, the city had been destroyed during the War of Two Brothers. Pizarro and his men marched toward Cajamarca. The Incan leader Atahuallpa was camped there. As the Spanish climbed the twisting mountain paths, the Inca could have easily attacked them. They did not. The Spaniards camped at night near the Incan storehouses, where the Inca treated the Spanish as guests. Atahuallpa probably did not think that an army of 177 men and 67 horses would try to conquer his empire.

On November 15, 1532, Pizarro entered Cajamarca. He sent word to Atahuallpa that he wanted to talk to him. Atahuallpa visited Pizarro with 6,000 men. None of the Inca carried weapons. A Spanish priest demanded that the Inca become **Christians**. Atahuallpa refused. Pizarro directed his soldiers to attack. Between 3,000 and 4,000 Inca were killed. Atahuallpa was taken prisoner.

Pizarro and Atahuallpa

While Atahuallpa was a Spanish prisoner he learned that the Spaniards wanted gold above all. The supreme Inca offered Pizarro a deal. If Pizarro freed him, Atahuallpa would fill one room with gold and another room twice with silver. Witnesses signed a contract because neither Pizarro nor Atahuallpa could write. Atahuallpa gave orders to his people to start collecting gold and silver. By June 1533, Pizarro had 13,420 pounds (6,087 kg) of gold and 26,000 pounds (11,793 kg) of silver. All Pizarro's men got shares of the gold. Because Diego de Almagro had not helped capture Atahuallpa, Pizarro did not give him a share. Instead Pizarro gave Almagro a small fee.

Despite his promise Pizarro did not free Atahuallpa. On July 26, Atahuallpa was put on trial for treason against the Spanish. He was found guilty and was **executed** the next day. Pizarro had one of Atahuallpa's brothers, Tupac Huallpa, crowned as the new supreme Inca. However, the Spanish also held Tupac Huallpa as a prisoner.

In this 1500s picture, the Inca bring gold to the Spanish conquerors. They hoped that with this payment the Spanish would release Atahuallpa. The Inca did not value gold because it was worth money. They valued it because for them it represented, or stood for, the "sweat of the Sun." Silver was valued because it represented the "tears of the Moon."

This toucan bird was made by an Incan artist sometime between 1400 and 1534. The bird is made from gold and turquoise, a blue-green gem.

While Atahuallpa was being held prisoner, his huge army could have attacked the Spaniards and tried to set Atahuallpa free. They could also have kept food from getting to the Spaniards. No Inca, though, was allowed to do anything without orders from the supreme Inca. Since Pizarro controlled the supreme Inca, no one could help Atahuallpa.

19

Fighting for Control

The Incan generals did not consider Tupac Huallpa the supreme Inca and decided to fight the Spaniards. The battles took place on flat ground. On flat ground the Spaniards' horses gave them an advantage. By around the end of 1534, the Spaniards had **defeated** all of Atahuallpa's generals. Two years later, however, the Inca attacked Cuzco, the Incan capital. On May 6, 1536, they trapped the Spaniards, who were led by Francisco Pizarro's brothers Hernando and Gonzalo.

Meanwhile, King Charles V had finally given Diego de Almagro, Pizarro's partner, his own territory. Almagro's territory turned out to be worth much less than Pizarro's territory. In April 1537, Almagro arrived in Cuzco, which he thought should be his. He drove the Indians from the city and jailed Pizarro's brothers. Gonzalo escaped. Pizarro promised that if Almagro freed Hernando, Almagro could keep Cuzco until King Charles V decided who should own it. Almagro agreed.

Timeline

Around 1475 Francisco Pizarro is born in Trujillo, Spain.

Between 1502 and 1509 Pizarro moves to Hispaniola.

1510 Alonso de Ojeda leaves Pizarro in charge of San Sebastián.

1513 Pizarro travels with Vasco Núñez de Balboa on the expedition during which Balboa discovers the Pacific Ocean.

1522 Pizarro and two partners decide to try to find Peru.

1527 Pizarro finds Peru. He does not have enough men to conquer it.

1528 Pizarro sails to Spain to get a license from King Charles V to conquer Peru.

1532 Pizarro captures the supreme Inca, Atahuallpa, in Peru.

1533 Pizarro agrees to free Atahuallpa if the Inca bring enough gold and silver. Pizarro has Atahuallpa killed.

1534 The Spaniards defeat the last of Atahuallpa's generals.

1536 The Inca attack the city of Cuzco and trap the Spaniards, including Pizarro's brothers Hernando and Gonzalo, inside.

153 Almagro drives away the Indians who had trapped the Spaniards in Cuzco. Then he throws Pizarro's brothers in prison.

1538 Pizarro goes to war with Almagro. Pizarro wins. Almagro is executed.

1541 Some of Almagro's men kill Pizarro after storming his palace in Lima.

This page is from a 1534 French book called Nouuelles certaines des Isles du Peru, *which means* Reports from the Islands of Peru. *The book has letters, which were first written in Spanish, from Pizarro and others about their discoveries. Pizarro could not write, so he told someone else what to record.*

From **Nouuelles certaines des Isles du Peru**

"Hereafter follow the letters of Francisco Pizarro, governor of that rich country and province called Peru, which mention those marvelous things seen not only by his own eyes but also through the letters sent to him by those who live in this same country which mention many new things not only of inestimable richness of gold, silver and precious stones found and taken in this province and country but also of other merchandise and richness . . ."

This means that the reader of this book would learn about Peru and its riches from the letters written by Pizarro and others.

21

Pizarro's Death

Francisco Pizarro did not keep his promise to Almagro. After Hernando was freed, Pizarro went to war with Almagro and defeated him. Almagro was executed. On June 26, 1541, some of Almagro's men stormed into Pizarro's palace in Lima and killed him.

Pizarro was a brave man who went through terrible times in his search for Peru. He was one of the most successful soldiers ever. Pizarro was so successful, though, because he lied and killed people who could not **defend** themselves. In 1542, the year after Pizarro was killed, Bartolomé de Las Casas wrote a book about the horrible way the Spaniards had mistreated the Native Americans. Around the same time, the Spaniards learned how Pizarro had also mistreated the Incan leader Atahuallpa. Although the Spaniards in Europe liked having the Inca's gold, they were ashamed of the way Pizarro got it. However, this shame would not prevent Europeans from sending other people to explore, conquer, and colonize the rich lands of the New World.

Glossary

Christians (KRIS-chunz) People who follow the teachings of Jesus Christ and the Bible.

colony (KAH-luh-nee) A new place where people move that is still ruled by the leaders of the country from which they came.

conquer (KON-ker) To take over something completely.

defeated (dih-FEET-ed) To have won against someone in a game or battle.

defend (dih-FEND) To guard from harm.

disease (duh-ZEEZ) An illness or sickness.

empire (EM-pyr) A large area controlled by one ruler.

excited (ik-SY-ted) Stirred up.

executed (EK-suh-kyoot-ed) To be put to death.

expedition (ek-spuh-DIH-shun) A trip for a special purpose.

explorer (ek-SPLOR-ur) A person who travels and looks for new land.

fort (FORT) A strong building or place that can be guarded against an enemy.

guilty (GIL-tee) Having done wrong.

harbor (HAR-ber) A protected body of water where ships anchor.

isthmus (IS-mus) A narrow strip of land connecting two larger bodies of land.

license (LY-suns) Official permission to do something.

partner (PART-ner) Two or more people who work together.

rebellion (ruh-BEL-yun) A fight against one's government.

settlers (SET-lerz) People who move to a new land to live.

shipwrecked (SHIP-rekd) When someone is left without a means of travel after his or her ship has been ruined, or destroyed.

supreme (suh-PREEM) Greatest in power or rank.

treason (TREE-zun) The crime of doing something that will hurt a king or queen or harm a government.

trial (TRYL) When a case is decided in court.

voyage (VOY-ij) A journey, especially by water.

Index

Web Sites

Due to the changing nature of Internet links, PowerKids Press has developed an online list of Web sites related to the subject of this book. This site is updated regularly. Please use this link to access the list.

http://www.powerkidslinks.com/pslfe/pizarro/

Primary Sources

Page 5. Top. Francisco Pizarro (detail). Portrait. 1500s. Anonymous. Museo de America, Madrid, Spain. **Page 6. Top.** World Map (detail). Circa 1544. From an atlas by Battista Agnese. Geography and Map Division, Library of Congress, Washington, D.C. **Page 6. Bottom.** The Spanish Attack the Indians. Engraving. 1602. From *Historia Americae*. (Latin for *History of America*). By Theodore de Bry. Biblioteca Nazionale Marciana, Venice, Italy. **Page 10. Top.** *Coast from Punta de Tascama to Island of Gorgonilla* (detail). Circa 1685. By William Hack. British Library, London, United Kingdom. A copy of a map Bartholomew Sharp, a pirate, stole from Spanish sailors in 1681. **Page 10. Bottom.** Pizarro, Almagro, and Luque Agree to Explore Peru. Engraving. 1596. From *Americae*, Part VI. By Theodore de Bry. Kunstbibliothek, Staatliche Museen zu Berlin, Berlin, Germany. **Page 12. Inset.** Pizarro and Almagro in Castile. Illustration. Circa 1587. From *Nueva corónica y buen gobierno*. (Spanish for *New Chronicle and Good Government*). By Felipe Guaman Poma de Ayala. Archeological Museum, Lima, Peru. **Page 12.** Pizarro Speaks to Charles V. Engraving. 1596. From *Americae*, Part VI. By Theodore de Bry. Kunstbibliothek, Staatliche Museen zu Berlin, Berlin, Germany. **Page 15. Bottom.** Atahuallpa (detail). Portrait. 1500s. Anonymous. Ethnologisches Museum, Staatliche Museen zu Berlin, Berlin, Germany. **Page 16. Left.** Atahuallpa in Chains. Illustration. Circa 1587. From *Nueva corónica y buen gobierno*. By Felipe Guaman Poma de Ayala. Archeological Museum, Lima, Peru. **Page 16. Right.** Atahuallpa and His Warriors. Engraving. 1596. From *Americae*, Part VI. By Theodore de Bry. Kunstbibliothek, Staatliche Museen zu Berlin, Berlin, Germany. **Page 19. Top.** The Inca Try to Ransom Atahuallpa. Engraving. 1602. From *Historia Americae*. By Theodore de Bry. Biblioteca Nazionale Marciana, Venice, Italy. **Page 21.** Start of *Nouvelles Certaines des Isles du Peru* (detail). (French for *Reports from the Islands of Peru*). 1534. Printed in Lyon. New York Public Library, New York, NY.